Can It Fit?

Written by Myleen Rush
Illustrated by Gloria Leek

Phonics Skill

Consonant Ll /l/

Lil	lid	lap
lit	doll	

Tab sat on a lap.
Kit did not.

Lil lit it.
Do you see Tab?

Lil had a doll.
Kit can bat it.

Kit sat in the lid.
Can Tab fit?

They fit in that lid.

Can Tab fit on Lil?
Can Kit fit on Lil?

They are on Lil.